ANN H. JUDSON

ANN H. JUDSON
OF BURMA

by E.R. PITMAN

CHRISTIAN LITERATURE CRUSADE
Fort Washington, Pennsylvania 19034

CHRISTIAN LITERATURE CRUSADE

U.S.A.
Box 1449, Fort Washington, PA 19034

CANADA
Box 189, Elgin, Ontario KOG 1EO

Copyright© 1936
Pickering & Inglis. Ltd.

First Edition 1936
This Edition 1974
This printing 1988
by special arrangement
with the British publisher.

ISBN 0-87508-601-2

PRINTED IN THE UNITED STATES OF AMERICA

Contents

1

Early Years

ANN HASSELTINE JUDSON, wife of the renowned "Judson of Burma," was one of the bravest foreign missionaries who ever lived—a frail woman who dared to venture with the gospel into a hostile, heathen land. She may also be regarded as the first woman missionary of modern times to foreign lands, the pioneer of mission effort by her sex. On this account an imperishable halo surrounds her life and memory. She lived, labored, and suffered for the gospel in the heathen country of Burma at a time when that country was under the awful regime of a barbarian and a bloodthirsty tyrant, when the country was in a ferment, when government was deranged, and when crime and murder were rife

Mrs. Judson and her companion Mrs. Harriet Newell were, we believe, the *very first* ladies who ventured on going to heathen lands as heralds of the gospel to their dark-skinned sisters. An early grave—in fact before mission work could be commenced—was allotted to Mrs. Newell; but the subject of this memoir lived, labored, and suffered for the gospel in no common degree for many years. No compendium of feminine missionary biography would be complete without a notice of Mrs. Ann Judson, and no chronicle of self-denying efforts can excel that furnished by the plain, unvarnished record of her life.

Mrs. Judson was an American by birth, having been born at Bradford, Massachusetts, on December 22, 1789. We are told that from her earliest years she was distinguished for activity of mind, extreme gaiety, a strong relish for social amusements, unusually ardent feelings, a spirt of enterprise, and restless, indefatigable perseverance. This restless spirit, in girlhood, was often the cause of uneasiness to her mother, Mrs. Hasseltine, so that on one occasion this lady said to Ann, "I hope, my daughter, you will one day be satisfied with rambling." Her eager thirst for knowledge was probably, however, the cause of her restless, enterprising disposition. She was fond of study, and attained distinction in the Academy at Bradford where she received her education. It was accepted as an indisputable conclusion by her preceptors and associates in this academy, that Miss Hasseltine's talents and temperaments foreshadowed some destiny of an uncommon character; and her after-career abundantly verified this early expectation of her.

Miss Hasseltine first became subject to serious impressions in her seventeenth year. By a variety of experiences and influences she was then led to feel the necessity for a change of heart, and to resolve to live a new life. At first, while seeing these things but dimly, she dreamt of procuring salvation by her own good works, and endeavored to live what she called "a religious life," so as to fit herself for heaven. She records, however, with much clearness, the difficulties which surrounded her, and how she was finally led to come to Christ, the true way of salvation. After many conflicts, and much prayerful seeking of the Lord Jesus, she found peace to her soul, and was able to rejoice in a sense of pardon. She realized fully the meaning of that striking fifth verse in the fourth chapter of the Epistle to the Romans: "To him that worketh not, but believeth on Him [Christ] that justifieth the ungodly, his faith is reckoned for righteousness." She had been working and doing when Christ had *finished the work,* and had done it all, and now she ceased *doing* and simply *believed*. It was believe and live—life first, then works; salvation first, then service. And, having truly believed on the Son of God, her life thereafter was spent in goodly works and noble service to her Master and Lord whom she loved and worshiped.

From the time of her conversion she strove to live according to the principles and promptings of the new life, doing whatever Christian service lay to her hand as far as opportunity and fitness suggested. The entries in her diary show that she "kept her heart with all diligence," and from her correspondence with intimate friends it appears that her growth in grace and self-knowledge was very marked. Some scattered observations will amply prove this. Such as, for instance:

"A person who grows in grace will see more and more of the dreadful wickedness of his own heart."

"The more grace Christians have, the more clearly they can see the contrast between holiness and sin. This will necessarily lead them to pray more often, earnestly, and fervently, give them a disrelish for the vanities of the world, and a sincere and hearty desire to devote all they have to Christ and to serve Him entirely."

"Growth in grace will lead Christians to know more about Jesus Christ, and the great need they have of Him for a whole Saviour."

About the age of eighteen she commenced teaching in a school, and filled engagements in this department of work at Salem, Haverhill, and Newbury, following the occupation with much success for some years. When twenty she obtained a copy of the *Life of David Brainerd,* and was stirred by it to consider the condition of the heathen world. She records in her diary that she "felt a willingness to give herself away to Christ, to be disposed of as He pleases." But the event which finally determined the nature of her future career was her betrothal to Adoniram Judson, who was then seeking to go to India as a foreign missionary.

A brief sketch of the early life of Adoniram Judson, the young man who was destined to become the "Apostle to Burma," would not be out of place at this juncture, so that will occupy our next chapter.

2

Adoniram Judson

STANDING OUT in history, like a beacon light amidst the dark days of religious intolerance, is the moving account of the departure from England of the Pilgrim Fathers, who sought in the new world across the Atlantic, now known as the United States, a new home and the liberty which was denied them in their own land.

Fourteen years after, in the year 1634, there followed William Judson, a Yorkshireman, who, taking with him his three sons, Joseph, Jeremiah, and Joshua, emigrated to the new land of America. The Biblical names indicate the Puritan home in Yorkshire, which was abandoned to be set up at Stratford, Connecticut. Through the son Joseph descended Adoniram Judson, who became a Congregational minister and married a godly woman named Abigail Brown.

Soon after his marriage he settled in the little village of Malden, Massachusetts, which one day was to become the historic starting point of the great War of Independence, and here his eldest son was born, and also named Adoniram, and he it was who became the famous missionary.

Above the average height, the father was a man of decidedly imposing appearance. Tall, erect, and grave in manner, when age had whitened his hair his venerable figure was an admirable study for a portrait of one of the old Pilgrim Fathers. The boy's affection for his father must have been deeply tinged with awe, for Mr. Judson was very strict in his domestic administrations, though a man of inflexible integrity and uniform consistency of Christian character.

Young Adoniram early gave promise of unusual ability. Amiable in temper, his intellect was acute, his power of acquisition great, and his perseverance unflagging. Self-reliant, he generally became acknowledged leader in the circles in which he moved.

At the age of three, while his father was away from home on a short journey, the mother, wishing to surprise her husband, took the opportunity to teach her boy to read. To the astonishment of the father on his return, he found that the child was able to read through a chapter of the Bible.

Early premonition was given of his future life work, for when he was in his fourth year he used to collect the children of the neighborhood, and standing on a chair before them, gravely conduct a religious service.

About this time his sister Abigail was born, whom he greatly loved. She was the companion of his childhood; into her ear he poured all his confidences, and she became his life-long confidante. Vivid reminiscences of his young days have been left by his sister, and we will readily cull certain brief extracts from her illuminating pen as occasion requires.

Adoniram was about seven years old when, having been duly instructed that the earth is a spherical body, and that it revolves around the sun, it became a serious question in his mind whether or not the sun moved at all. He might have settled the point by asking his father or mother, but that would have spoiled all his pleasant speculations, and probably would have been the last thing to occur to him. His little sister, whom he alone consulted, said the sun did move, for she said she could see it; but he had learned already, in this matter, to distrust the evidence of his senses, and he talked so wisely about positive proof that she was astonished and silenced. Soon after this he was one day missed about midday; and as he had not been seen for several hours, his father became uneasy, and went in search of him. He was found in a field, at some distance from the house, stretched on his back, his hat with a circular hole cut in the crown laid over his face, and his swollen eyes almost blinded with the intense light and heat. He only told his father that he was looking at the sun; but he assured his sister that he had solved the problem with regard to the sun's moving, though she never could comprehend the process by which he arrived at the result.

"He was noted," as his sister comments, "for uncommon acuteness in the solution of charades and enigmas, and retained a great store of them in his memory for the purpose of puzzling his schoolfellows. He had also gained quite a reputation for good scholarship, especially in arithmetic. A gentleman residing in a neighbouring town sent him a problem with the offer of a dollar for the solution. Adoniram immediately shut himself in his chamber. The reward was tempting, but more important still, his reputation was at stake. On the morning of the second day he was called from his seclusion to amuse his little brother, who was ill. He went reluctantly, but without murmuring, for the government of his parents was of a nature that no child would think of resisting. His task was to build a cob house. He laid an unusually strong foundation, with unaccountable slowness and hesitation, and was deliberately proceeding with the superstructure when suddenly he exclaimed, 'That's it! I've got it!' and sending the materials for the half-built house rolling about the room, he hurried off to his chamber to record the result. The problem was solved, the dollar was won, and the boy's reputation established."

At the age of ten he took lessons in navigation, and at the grammar school became so proficient in the Greek language that his schoolmates nicknamed him

"Virgil." At twelve, he attempted to procure and study a learned exposition of the Book of Revelation, but his father wisely procured other books instead for one so young.

Adoniram's mental capacity was developed beyond his years, and in his passion for study it is not to be wondered at that his assiduous poring over books brought the inevitable breakdown. At this time his studies were interrupted by a serious illness; he was reduced to a state of extreme weakness, and for a long time his recovery was doubtful. His illness does not appear to have been due to anything lacking in his constitution, but simply because of his studious habits. All books and studies had to be laid aside, and for twelve months he was unable to pursue his customary occupations. Because of his incessant study he had not given much time to thought, but now in his enfeebled state, unable to read, he had ample time for reflection. And in his long dreary days he mused over the plans and course of his future career. Great were his plans and extravagant his ambitions, but this should hardly surprise us from one of such a studious character. Lying there in his room, he built his castles and soared high. The remarkable flights of his imagination and his outlook upon life during this period have been preserved, and we have mirrored for us the workings of his mind.

"Now he was an orator, now a poet, now a statesman, but whatever his character or profession, he was sure in his castle building to attain to the highest eminence. His father had said that one day he would become a great man, and a great man he resolved to be."

Yes, he was to be a great man, but not in the manner he now anticipated. Marvelous are the ways of God in dealing with us, and this choice soul was yet to learn the worthlessness of worldly ambition and to be guided into God's channel to fulfil His plan and purpose.

As the days slowly passed he recovered his old strength, and when sixteen entered Providence College, now Brown University. Twelve months' leeway had now to be made up, and he was obliged to devote himself very closely to his studies, and seldom gave himself any respite, even during the vacations. Ambitious to excel, he was a hard student.

The seeds of infidelity, the production of the French Revolution, had just then been wafted across the ocean and scattered throughout the land, producing their evil crop of tares, and an amiable and talented classmate of Judson's had imbibed these infidel ideas. Between them a strong friendship sprang up, and during the days they were together the infidel notions came up for discussion. They also often reverted to the subject of a profession, considering the scope for their ambitions in the drama. The influence of this fascinating personality had its evil effects upon the youth, so far safeguarded from infidel ideas, and resulted in young Judson becoming, or at least professedly so, as great an unbeliever as his friend.

After graduating with a Bachelor of Arts degree, Adoniram determined on gaining a real experience of life, to see the dark side of the world as well as the bright. Arriving in New York he attached himself to a theatrical company, though for no particular reason.

A few nights later he stopped at a country inn to find the only accommodation to be had was a room next to one in which a young man lay dying. On rising next morning, he learned that the sick man had died. Enquiring who he was, Adoniram was stunned to discover that he was his infidel classmate. This tragic event so wrought on him that he abandoned his tour and returned to Plymouth.

At this crisis two professors in the Theological Seminary at Andover visited Adoniram's father, and proposed to him that his son should enter that seminary. Adoniram did not at first consent to the proposal, and engaged himself as an assistant to a teacher. This situation, however, he soon relinquished, and proceeded to Andover to enter the seminary. As he was neither a professing Christian, nor a candidate for the ministry, he was admitted only by special favor.

At this time he had not found forgiveness through Christ. He had become thoroughly dissatisfied with the views which he had formerly cherished, and was convicted of his sinfulness and his need of a great moral transformation. Yet he doubted the authenticity of revealed religion, and clung to the deistic ideas

which he had lately imbibed. His mind did not readily yield to the force of evidence, but his is by no
means an uncommon case; nor is it difficult of expla-
nation. A deep-seated dislike to the humbling doc-
trines of the Cross frequently assumes the form of
inability to apply the common principles of evidence
to the case of revealed religion.

Adoniram's moral nature was, however, thoroughly roused, and he was deeply in earnest on
the subject of religion. The professors of the seminary encouraged his residence there, wisely judging
that so diligent an inquirer must soon arrive at the
truth. The result justified their anticipations. In the
calm retirement of Andover, guided in his studies by
men of learning and piety, with nothing to distract his
attention from the great concerns of eternity, light
gradually dawned upon his mind, and he was enabled
to surrender his whole soul to Christ as his Saviour
and Lord.

The change wrought in Adoniram Judson was
deep and real. With simplicity of purpose he yielded
himself up once and for ever to the will of God, and
without a shadow of misgiving relied upon Christ as
his all-sufficient Saviour. From the moment of his
conversion he seems never through life to have been
harassed by a doubt of his acceptance. His one ambition now was to "walk worthy of the Lord unto all
pleasing."

At the age of twenty-one he began to consider
seriously the subject of foreign missions, mainly

through reading a sermon entitled *The Star in the East,* by Dr. Buchanan, formerly a chaplain of the East India Company. His thoughts were finally turned to Burma by reading Colonel Syme's *Embassy to Ava,* though he did not think exclusively of that country. Five other students, Mills, Richards, Rice, Hall, and Nott, of like aspirations, constituted themselves a missionary society and resolved to leave their native land to engage in missionary work as soon as providential openings should appear. There being then no suitable Foreign Missionary Society in the United States, these young men determined to seek English help and direction in the matter, unless a society could be formed.

An appeal was made by Mr. Judson and his fellow-students to the Congregational body of America for direction and support. None being immediately forthcoming, Mr. Judson sailed for England, to confer with the Directors of the London Missionary Society, with the result that this Society agreed to maintain him and his colleagues, provided the American Board of Missions could not, or would not, do so. Having obtained this promise, he returned home.

And here we leave the brilliant young Adoniram Judson to speak more particularly of the subject of our sketch, the noble young lady who was to become his wife.

A young man from the Shan States of Burma

3

The Double Proposal

IN SEPTEMBER, 1811, the American Board of Missions decided to establish a mission in Burma, and appointed Messrs. Judson, Nott, Newell, and Hall as their first missionary agents. Immediately his life course was thus determined, Mr. Judson made an offer of marriage to Miss Hasseltine, whom he had first met some little time previously.

In a frank, manly letter to her father he wrote asking his consent to their marriage, and like Abraham of old, this godly father yielded up his loved one at the call of God.

Mr. Judson was equally frank to Miss Hasseltine, so that she might arrive at a decision fully understanding what was involved, and in a letter to her from which we quote, he forecasts the future.

"May this be the year in which you will change your name; in which you will take final leave of your relatives and native land; in which you will cross the wide ocean and dwell on the other side of the world among a heathen people. What a great change will this year probably effect in our lives! How very different will be our situation and employment! If our lives are preserved and our attempt prospered, we shall next new year's day be in India and perhaps wish each other a happy new year in the uncouth dialect of Hindustan or Burma. We shall no more see our friends around us, or enjoy the conveniences of civilised life, or go to the house of God with those that keep holy days; but swarthy countenances will everywhere meet our eyes, the jargon of an unknown tongue will assail our ears, and we shall witness the assembling of heathen to celebrate the worship of idol gods. We shall be weary of the world, and wish for wings like a dove that we may fly away and be at rest. We shall probably experience seasons when we shall be 'exceeding sorrowful even unto death.' We shall see many dreary, disconsolate hours, and feel a sinking of spirits, and anguish of mind, of which now we can form little conception . O, we shall wish to lie down and die, and that time may soon come! One of us may be unable to sustain the heat of the climate and the change of habits; and the other may say, with literal truth, over the grave:

'By foreign hands thy dying eyes were closed;
By foreign hands thy decent limbs composed;
By foreign hands thy humble grave adorned.'

But whether we shall be honoured and mourned by strangers, God only knows. At least, either of us will be certain of one mourner. In view of such scenes, shall we not pray with earnestness, 'O for overcoming faith!' "

Miss Hasseltine carefully considered Mr. Judson's proposal of marriage, and gave herself to prayer and much heart-searching. It was not easy to decide, as the proposition, which in itself was sufficiently momentous and important, was made doubly so when linked with the idea of spending herself for Christ in heathen lands. She had no example to guide her, and no prospect at this time of having any female companion in the mission field. She fully realized the many sacrifices that she would be called upon to make, and felt the need of being convinced that this was a call of God. Her many friends opposed the undertaking as wild and visionary.

One lady friend said to another, "I hear that Miss Hasseltine is going to India! Why does she go?"

"Why, she thinks it to be her duty! Would you not go if you thought it your duty?"

"But," replied the lady, "*I would not think it my duty!*"

And more than all conflicting opinions was the remembrance and consideration of the fact that *no woman* had, as yet, ever left American shores to engage in mission work. It always takes strong faith to be a pioneer. One cannot appeal to precedents, or examples, and so is forced to stand firmly upon convictions of duty and divine command. These, with providential indications of guidance and leading, constituted all that Miss Hasseltine could fall back upon wherewith to meet the objections of enemies, or the well-intentioned dissuasions of friends. Her path, in common with all those godly women who obeyed the Lord's summons into the mission field at that day, was infinitely harder and darker than that of any of her own sex who now depart in such numbers for mission work among the native women and children. The novelty is worn off, it is true, in great measure; but with this, the risk is gone, and the wide gulf which formerly existed between those who went to heathen lands and those who remained at home has been bridged over, so that unmarried ladies now dare to go where their married sisters at first trod with feeble and hesitating footsteps.

That spirit of enterprise and adventure which had always distinguished Miss Hasseltine now came out, and stood her in good stead. She decided to go; and thus earned the honorable distinction of being *the first American lady* to engage in foreign-mission work. Indeed, it seems not incorrect to say that Mrs. Judson was *the first lady missionary,* whether America or Europe be considered, for Mrs. Moffat, Mrs. Williams, Mrs. Krapf, Mrs. Gobat, and other eminent lady toilers in the mission field, were all later in point of time.

Writing of her decision, Miss Hasseltine says: "Might I but be the means of converting a single soul, it would be worth spending all my days to accomplish. Yes, I feel willing to be placed in that situation in which I can do most good, though it were to carry the Gospel to the distant benighted heathen. A consideration of this subject has occasioned much self-examination to know on what my hopes were founded, and whether my love to Jesus was sufficiently strong to induce me to forsake all for His cause. At other times I feel ready to sink, and appalled at the prospect of pain and suffering to which my nature is so averse and apprehensive. But I have at all times felt a disposition to leave it with God, and trust in Him to direct me. I have at length come to the conclusion that if nothing in providence appears to prevent I must spend my days in a heathen land. I am a creature of God, and He has an undoubted right to do with me as seemeth good in His sight. He has my heart in His hands, and when I am called to face danger, to pass through scenes of terror and distrust, He can inspire me with fortitude, and enable me to trust in Him. Jesus is faithful, His promises are precious. Were it not for these considerations, I should, with my present prospects, sink down in despair, especially as no woman has, to my knowledge, ever left the shores of America to spend her life among the heathen. But God is my witness that I have not dared to decline the offer that has been made to me, though so many are ready to call it 'a wild, romantic undertaking.' . . . I am not only willing to spend my days among the heathen, in attempting to enlighten and save them, but I find much pleasure in the prospect. Yes, I am quite willing to give up temporal comforts, and live a life of hardship and trial, if it be the will of God."

Yes, the decision was made, and Ann Hasseltine yielded herself to God for His great work.

A Burmese sailing craft

4

Departure for Burma

MR. AND MRS. JUDSON were married on the 5th of February, 1812, and on the next day Messrs. Newell, Nott, Hall, Rice, and Judson were bid Godspeed by friends, in the Tabernacle Church, Salem, Massachusetts. Messrs. Judson and Newell, with their newly-married wives, sailed from Salem on the 19th of February, in the brig *Caravan* for Calcutta, amid the tearful "God-speeds" of their friends and relatives; mingling with the benisons of others upon their unwonted and perilous enterprise. The voyage presented the usual incidents only, and although suffering much from sea-sickness, Mrs. Judson sustained a buoyant faith and a Christian deportment, improving the time in reading and studying works calculated to fit her for the arduous duties awaiting her. Their long voyage ended on the 17th of June, they having been afloat on the billows for four unpleasant and weary months.

Landing at Calcutta on the 18th of June, they were welcomed by the venerable Dr. Carey, who immediately invited them to his mission quarters at Serampore, there to reside until their companions should reach India, and their future movements should be settled. After staying one night in Calcutta, therefore, they took a boat and proceeded up the river some fifteen miles to Serampore, the headquarters of the Baptist English Mission. Messrs. Carey, Marshman, and Ward were then residing with their families under Danish protection, for the British Government of that day, influenced by powerful trading concerns, was opposed to missionaries and mission operations. Dr. Carey was busily at work upon his translation of the Scriptures; Dr. Marshman and his family were engaged in educational work, and Mr. Ward was superintending the printing operations of the mission.

From a letter to her sister the following remarks are extracted. They will serve to show Mrs. Judson's first impressions on entering Eastern lands. Speaking of Dr. Carey's house, she says: "His house is curiously constructed, as the other European houses are here. There are no chimneys or fireplaces in them. The roofs are flat, the rooms are twenty feet in height, and proportionally large. Large windows without glass open from one room to another that the air may freely circulate through the house. They are very convenient for this climate, and bear every mark of antiquity. In the evening we attended service in the English Episcopal Church. It was our first attendance at Divine service for about four months, and as we entered the church our ears were delighted with hearing the organ play our favourite tune 'Bangor.' The church was very handsome, and a number of punkahs, something like fans several yards in length, hung around with ropes fastened to the outside, which were pulled by some of the natives to keep the church cool. Very near the house is a school, supported by this mission, in which are instructed two hundred boys, and nearly as many girls. They are chiefly children of Portuguese parents, and natives of no caste. We could see them all kneel at prayer-time, and hear them sing at the opening of the school."

The mission life of the settlement was pleasant and bracing, but it was not to last. They had been there only about ten days when a Government order arrived summoning Messrs. Judson and Newell to Calcutta. They went, and on their arrival at the seat of Government an order was read to them requiring them immediately to leave India and return to America. All students of missionary annals well know that the old East India Company, which then ruled India, was vehemently opposed to the introduction of Christianity among the natives. The Company professed to believe that the natives would be offended by the introduction of a new religion; but the truth is that a good revenue was brought in from such shocking spectacles as the Feast of Juggernaut.

The Company were most reluctant to give educational advantages to the natives, and the disgraceful treatment of the natives by the Company's officials would present a glaring contrast to the godly lives and compassionate treatment of the missionaries. The opposition to the American missionaries was also intensified because England and America at that time were not on friendly relations. But in 1813 the Charter of the Company required to be renewed, and the friends of missions in the British Parliament, such as Wilberforce, Thornton, and Smith, mustered all their influence to secure toleration for missionaries and their work. Having succeeded in their noble effort, the English possessions were constituted into a bishopric, Dr. Middleton being the first bishop. He was succeeded by good Reginald Heber, author of the well-known hymn commencing, "From Greenland's Icy Mountains"; and ever since this new departure taken by the Government, missionary operations have been safe and welcome. Indeed, to some of the Governor-Generals of India the Christian churches owe much gratitude for the noble manner in which the strong arm of the law has been exerted on behalf of humanity and religion.

But this order to depart out of the country did not constitute the Judsons' only difficulty. The American Board of Missions had ordered them to start a mission in Burma, unless circumstances should render it *impossible* to attempt it. The Serampore missionaries were united in thinking that it *was* impossible, both considering the despotic nature of the Burmese Government and the failure of all preceding attempts to introduce the gospel there. Under such united discouragements, it was decided to desist from the attempt, and Mr. Newell and his wife very soon set sail for the Isle of France, as the island of Mauritius was then called, where Mrs. Newell soon after passed away before really entering at all upon mission work. But Mr. and Mrs. Judson remained in Calcutta, quietly awaiting the issue of events.

While in the company of the Serampore missionaries, and also during the voyage out, Mr. Judson and his wife were led to change their sentiments in relation to the mode in which Christian baptism should be administered. They did not make this change without much and serious consideration; but having come to a decision they took the painful step of leaving the communion of American Congregational Churches, and joining the Baptists without question or delay. Indeed, had they considered the question of self-interest, profit, or ease of mind, they would not have added to their other difficulties at this eventful period by changing their baptismal views, or their religious denomination. They were not alone in this change of opinion seeing that some of their missionary companions also adopted Baptist views.

Their connection with the American Board of Missions for the Congregational Churches was thereafter considered dissolved. But as yet they were not connected with any Baptist Society, and while the Serampore missionaries were all that could be desired, it was obviously impossible for them to remain there. All that seemed certain was the fact that they must quickly leave India, or be shipped from there by force. Yet they were ready to go anywhere could any position or any promise of support be forthcoming. At one time Mr. Judson thought of going to South America, and commenced learning Portuguese in order for this move. Japan, Persia, Madagascar, and Burma were all considered, seriously and prayerfully, as possible fields in which to commence missionary effort, while waiting for providential direction.

The following extract from a letter written to a friend by Mrs. Judson proves to what great straits they were brought at this juncture. She says: "We had almost concluded to go to the Burmese Empire when we heard there were fresh difficulties existing between the British and Burmese Governments. If these difficulties are settled, I think it probable we shall go there. It presents a very extensive field for usefulness, containing seventeen millions of inhabitants, and the Scriptures have never been translated into their language. This circumstance is a very strong inducement to Mr. Judson to go there, as there is no other place where he could be equally useful in translating. But our privations and dangers would be great. There are no bread, potatoes, or butter, and very little of any animal food. The natives live principally on rice and fish. I should have no society at all except my husband, for there is not an English lady in all Rangoon. But I could easily give up these comforts if the Government were such as to secure safety to its subjects. But where our lives would depend on the caprice of a monarch, or on those who have the power of life and death, we could never feel safe unless we always had strong faith in God. Notwithstanding these difficulties, we are perfectly willing to go, if our dear Lord opens the way."

Meanwhile the Bengal Government were extremely incensed by the sojourn of the Mission Party in the country, supposing very likely that they intended to remain there. At the end of two months they therefore issued a most peremptory order to the effect that the little band were to be at once sent on board one of the East India Company's vessels, and shipped to England. Here was a dilemma! However, Messrs. Judson and Rice were equal to the occasion, and, having ascertained that a vessel named the *Creole* would sail for the Isle of France (Mauritius) in two days' time, they applied to the Government for a passport. This was refused. Then they told the captain their circumstances, and asked if he would take them without a passport. He replied that he would be neutral; there was his ship and they could do as they pleased. Under cover of night they boarded the vessel, but while sailing down the river they were overtaken by a Government dispatch who commanded the pilot to conduct the ship no farther as there were persons on board who had been ordered to England. They were forced to leave the ship, and took refuge in a tavern on shore. Feeling that it was not safe to remain there, they proceeded to another tavern sixteen miles farther down the river.

The following extract from a letter written by Mrs. Judson to her parents describes the incidents at this critical time:

"We had now given up all hope of going to the Isle of France, and concluded either to return to Calcutta or to communicate our real situation to the tavern keeper, and request him to assist us. As we thought the latter preferable, Mr. Judson told our landlord our circumstances, and asked him if he could assist in getting us a passage to Ceylon. He said a friend of his was expected down the river the next day, who was captain of a vessel bound for Madras, and who, he did not doubt, would take us. This raised our sinking hopes. We waited two days, and on the third, which was the Sabbath, the ship came in sight and anchored directly before the house. We now expected the time of our deliverance had come. The tavern keeper went on board to see the captain for us, but our hopes were again dashed when he returned and said the captain could not take us. We determined, however, to see the captain ourselves, and endeavour to persuade him to let us have a passage at any rate. We had just sat down to supper when a letter was handed to us. We hastily opened it, and, to our great surprise and joy, in it was a pass from the magistrate for us to go on board the *Creole,* the vessel we had left. Who procured this pass for us, or in what way, we are still ignorant of; we could only view the hand of God and wonder. But we had every reason to expect the *Creole* had got out to sea, as it was three days since we left her. There was a possibility, however, of her having anchored at Saugur, seventy miles from where we then were. We had let our baggage continue in the boat in which it was first taken, therefore it was all in readiness; and after dark we all got into the same boat, and set out against the tide for Saugur. It was a most dreary night to me, but Mr. Judson slept the greater part of the night. The next day we had a favourable wind, and before night reached Saugur, where were many ships at anchor, and among the rest we had the happiness to find the *Creole.* She had been anchored there for two days waiting for some of the ship's crew. I never enjoyed a sweeter moment in my life than that when I was sure we were in sight of the *Creole.* After spending a fortnight in such anxiety, it was a very great relief to find ourselves safe on board the vessel. All of us are now attending to the French language, as that is spoken altogether at the Isle of France. Though it has pleased our Heavenly Father to afflict us, yet He has supported and delivered us from our trials, which still encourages us to trust in Him."

Though difficulties defied them, yet were they not

daunted, and we cannot but feel the deepest admiration for this brave woman.

The passage was a long and stormy one, and after six weeks' sailing they arrived at Port Louis, Isle of France, on the 17th of January, 1813. Here they were met by Mr. Newell with the sad news of the death of his wife and baby girl, who had succumbed to the severe privations of the voyage. Thus died the first American woman martyr to foreign missions. It was not a promising or cheerful beginning for this new work, but gathering up their energies, they proceeded to study French, so as to be better fitted for mission work on the island. While the Judsons remained here, illness compelled Mr. Rice to return to America, and there he sought to awaken the interest of the Baptist churches in the work of foreign missions. As a result the Baptist General Convention was formed in Philadelphia, and one of the first acts of this Convention was to appoint Mr. and Mrs. Judson as their missionaries, leaving it to themselves to select a field of labor. Thus one great difficulty was cleared away.

After much consideration Mr. and Mrs. Judson resolved to go to Madras in the hope of obtaining a passage from thence to Penang, a town on the coast of Malacca, and inhabited by Malays. They took this step, reaching Madras in June, 1813. But here they were to experience fresh disappointments, for no vessel could be heard of bound to Penang. There was one, however, bound for Rangoon in Burma; and fearing a second expulsion from the country at the hands of the East India Company, Mr. Judson inquired the destination of vessels in the Madras roads. "I found none that would sail in season, but one bound to Rangoon. A mission to Rangoon we had been accustomed to regard with feelings of horror. But it was now brought to a point. We must either venture there or be sent to Europe. All other paths were shut up; and thus situated, though dissuaded by all our friends at Madras, we commended ourselves to the care of God." So, by a series of peculiar providences, they after all went to Burma. It was a remarkable illustration of the passage, "A man's heart deviseth his way, but the Lord directeth his steps" (Prov. 16:9).

But trials still dogged their course. A friendly European woman whom Mrs. Judson had engaged to go to Burma as her personal attendant fell suddenly dead on the deck just before the vessel sailed. Then the vessel was old and unseaworthy, and they experienced imminent peril of shipwreck in the storms which overtook them. Mrs. Judson herself was very ill, and as yet they had not entered on the special work they were sent from America to do, because of hindrances over which they had no control.

However, at last they arrived at Rangoon, and in this city of 40,000 inhabitants, "wholly given to idolatry," they took breath, preparatory to beginning work for Christ. The Serampore missionaries had attempted a mission there once, but had failed to make much impression upon the natives. One of the missionaries had translated the Gospel of Matthew into the Burman tongue, but it was not yet printed. The only two of the band who still remained were Mr. and Mrs. Felix Carey, and they welcomed Mr. and Mrs. Judson to their quaint little house. Mr. Carey was mainly employed by the Government, and he was confined to the city of Rangoon.

The country of Burma to which they had come is productive of all that is needed for food, clothing, and shelter. The chief crops are rice, corn, wheat, cotton, and indigo, while there is an abundance of delicious fruits—jackfruit, breadfruit, oranges, bananas, guavas, pineapples, and the coconut. The earth yields iron, tin, silver, gold, sapphires, emeralds, rubies, amber, sulphur, arsenic, antimony, coal, and petroleum, those precious minerals which bring the foreigner to the country in search of wealth.

Wild animals, such as the monkey, elephant, rhinoceros, tiger, leopard, deer, and wildcat, swarm in the jungles, while venomous reptiles and offensive insects abound.

The inhabitants of Burma belong to the Mongolian race, who are noted for their long, straight hair, almost complete absence of beard, a dark-colored skin, varying from a leather-like yellow to a deep brown, and prominent cheek bones. They are cheerful, and singularly alive to the ridiculous; buoyant and elastic, soon recovering from personal or domestic disaster. They are attached to their homes and children, are temperate and hardy, but idle, disliking constant employment or hard work, though this latter disability is by no means confined to the Burmese!

Writing home at this time, Mrs. Judson said: "We felt very gloomy and dejected the first night we arrived in view of our prospects, but we were enabled to lean on God, and to feel that He was able to support us under the most discouraging circumstances. The next morning I prepared to go ashore, but hardly knew how I should get to Mr. Carey's house, there being no method of conveyance except a horse, and I was unable to ride. It was, however, concluded that I should be carried in an armchair; consequently, when I landed, one was provided, through which were put two bamboos, and four of the natives took me on their shoulders. When they had carried me a little way into the town, they set me down under a shade, when great numbers of the natives gathered round, as they had seldom seen an Englishwoman. Being sick and weak, I held my head down, which induced many of the native women to come very near, and look under my bonnet. At this I looked up and smiled, at which they set up a loud laugh. They next carried me to a place they call the Custom House. After searching Mr. Judson very closely, they asked permission for a native woman to search me, to which I readily consented. I was then brought to the mission house, where I have entirely recovered my health."

One day Mrs. Judson visited the wife of the Viceroy of Rangoon, and we give her account of her reception:

"I was introduced to her by a French lady, who frequently visited her. When we first arrived at the Government House she was not up; consequently we had to wait some time. But the inferior wives of the Viceroy diverted us much by their curiosity in minutely examining everything we had on, and by trying on our gloves, bonnets, etc. At last her highness made her appearance, dressed richly in Burmese fashion, with a long silver pipe in her mouth, smoking. At her appearance, all the other wives took their seats at a respectful distance, and sat in a crouching posture, without speaking. She received me very politely, took me by the hand, seated me upon a mat, and herself by me. She excused herself for not coming in sooner, saying she was unwell. One of the women brought her a bunch of flowers, of which she took several and ornamented her cap. She was very inquisitive whether I had a husband and children; whether I was my husband's first wife, meaning by this whether I was the highest among them, supposing that my husband, like the Burmans, had many wives; and whether I intended tarrying long in the country. When the Viceroy came in I really trembled, for I never before beheld such a savage-looking creature. His long robe and enormous spear not a little increased my dread. He spoke to me, however, very condescendingly, and asked if I would drink some rum or wine. When I rose to go, her highness again took my hand; told me she was happy to see me, that I must come to see her every day, for I was like a sister to her. She led me to the door, and I made my salaam and departed."

Anxious to spare no time, Mrs. Judson began to study the language, and to mingle with the natives. Her former ideas of the ignorance and delusions of the Burmese people were in consequence deepened and intensified by what she saw and heard. Lying appeared to be universal, and it was common for them to say, "We cannot live without telling lies."

In regard to religion, they held the most absurd notions imaginable. As a case in point, Mrs. Judson's own teacher told her that whenever he died he should go to her own country—and this teacher was an able and intelligent man, far superior to the generality of his countrymen.

Among other things, the Burmese believed that there were four superior heavens; then below these, twelve other heavens, followed by six inferior heavens; after which followed the earth, the world of snakes, and then thirty-two chief hells; to which were to be added one hundred and twenty hells of milder torments. They were also taught that the lowest state of existence was hell; and the next was the form of brute-animals—both these being states of punishment. The next ascent was to that of man, which was probationary, and so on, up to demi-gods and full-blown deities. Happiness, or eternal absorption in Buddha, was to be obtained by works of merit; and among works of the highest merit was the feeding of a hungry, infirm tiger with a person's own flesh!

The study of the language proved a difficult task. It was exceedingly hard to master, and to add to the difficulty, there were no grammars or dictionaries, or other helps, such as are mostly enjoyed by modern students. The language itself was called "the Round O Language," and contained some syllables coinciding with the colloquial dialect of the Chinese. At that date the books were composed of the common palmyra leaf; but certain important documents were written on plates of gilded iron.

Specimen from a tract in Burman characters.

The above sample of the language, taken from a tract written by Mr. Judson some years later, will serve to show how difficult the task of acquiring it must have been.

Writing of her occupations at this time, Mrs. Judson says: "As it respects ourselves, we are busily employed all day long. I can assure you that we find much pleasure in our employment. Could you look into a large open room, which we call a verandah, you would see Mr. Judson bent over his table covered with Burman books, with his teacher at his side, a venerable-looking man in his sixtieth year, with a cloth wrapped round his middle, and a handkerchief round his head. They talk and chatter all day long, with hardly any cessation. My mornings are busily occupied in giving directions to the servants, providing food for the family, etc. At ten my teacher comes, when, were you present, you might see me in an inner room at one side of my study table, and my teacher at the other, reading Burman, writing, talking, etc. I have many more interruptions than Mr. Judson, as I have the entire management of the family. This I took upon myself, for the sake of Mr. Judson attending more closely to the study of the language; yet I have found, by a year's experience, that it was the most direct way I could have taken to acquire the language, as I am frequently obliged to speak Burman all day. I can talk to and understand the others better than Mr. Judson, though he knows more about the nature and construction of the language."

Speaking of privations, she writes thus to a friend: "As it respects our temporal privations, use has made them familiar and easy to be borne. They are of short duration, and, when brought into competition with the work of saving souls, sink into nothing. We have no society, no dear Christian friends, and, with the exception of two or three sea-captains who now and then call upon us, we never see a European face."

Planting out rice—Burma's major crop

5

Sowing the Seed

AFTER SIX MONTHS of residence and study in
Burma, Mrs. Judson's health gave way to such an
extent that she was obliged to sail for Madras in order
to procure medical treatment. After remaining in
that city some three months, and gaining much benefit, she returned again to Burma. Some things
occurred during this time which served to encourage
her. The Viceroy was so favorably impressed with
the missionary couple that he granted Mrs. Judson an
order to take a native woman with her to Madras, free
of expense—and this in spite of the Burmese law
which forbade any female to leave the country. The
captain of the vessel refused to take any fare for Mrs.
Judson's passage; and the physician at Madras refused to receive anything for his services, so that on
every hand she experienced unexpected kindness.
At the same time cheering signs appeared in connec-

tion with their work among the people, which hitherto was mostly conversational. The Burmese recognized the fact that the Judsons did not tell falsehoods, that they were to be depended upon, and that they always gave them kind treatment. Consequently they observed and listened attentively to the two pale-faced foreigners who had come from across the water to tell them of another and a better religion; and although they said again and again, "Your religion is good for you, ours for us; you will be rewarded for your good deeds in your way, and we in our way," they yet began to realize that in many essential points the religion of Jesus Christ was different from the religion of Buddha. There were also some very encouraging instances of inquirers seeking to know something more about this strange faith.

In May, 1816, their firstborn, a boy, aged eight months, was laid in the grave. This trial drew forth much sympathy from the wife of the Viceroy, who seems to have taken quite a liking to Mrs. Judson. She sometimes had opportunites of talking to this lady in the Government House, and did not fail to sow the seed of the gospel in simple language.

About this time the American Baptist Society sent out two additional missionaries to the assistance of the Judsons—Mr. and Mrs. Hough. This circumstance was very encouraging, for they had been laboring in loneliness and sorrow for three years without seeing much spiritual fruit of their labors. True, they had been laying foundations, and preparing them-

selves for future usefulness; but foundation work is
mostly work requiring faith, perseverance, and con-
stancy. Mr. Judson had written two tracts in the
language which were waiting to be printed and published. These tracts were soon after given to the
Burmese world by Mr. Hough, who was a practical
printer, and had brought with him a printing press,
types, and other apparatus, as a present from the
missionaries at Serampore. Experience had taught
them that although this mode of procedure was slow
it would prove to be the most effectual way ultimately of reaching the Burmese, for whenever anything was said to them on the subject of religion, they
would inquire for the missionaries' holy books. They
also found that most of the natives could read, and
entertained an almost superstitious reverence for
"the *written* doctrine." For these reasons Mr. Judson
concluded that it was now time to teach by means of
the printed page. Of the two small tracts printed, one
was a catechism of simple truths, and the other a
summary of Christian doctrine. Next, the missionaries determined to give the people some portion of the Scriptures.

One of the most memorable days in their lives was
a certain day in March, 1817, when Mr. Judson was
visited by the *first* inquirer after the Christian religion. And he was only the first of many who made the
same inquiries, though sometimes with subdued and
timid manner, as if afraid to let anyone suspect their
new interest. They gladly received copies of the two

little tracts already printed, and asked for "more of this sort of writing." Some of these inquirers passed out into the great world and were heard of no more, but others made, afterwards, a good confession of faith. At the same time Mrs. Judson formed a Sunday class for women for instruction in the Scriptures, for it had been long her ardent desire to lead some of her own sex in Burma to Christ. Her own account of this little society is graphic and interesting:

"How interested you would be, could you meet with my society of Burmese women on the Sabbath. Interested, do I say? Yes, you would be interested, if it was only from this circumstance—that these poor idolaters enjoy the means of grace, and sit under the sound of the Gospel. I have generally fifteen or twenty. They are attentive while I read the Scriptures, and endeavour to teach them about God. One of them told me the other day that she could not think of giving up a religion which her parents and grandparents held and accepting a new one, of which they had never heard. I asked her if she wished to be lost simply because her grandparents were? She replied, 'If with all her offerings and good works on her head, she must go to hell, then let her go.' I told her if she were lost after having heard of her Saviour, her very relations would contribute to torment her, and upbraid her for her rejection of that Saviour of whom they had never heard, and that even she herself would regret her folly when it was too late. 'If I do,' said she, 'I will then cry out to you to be my interces-

sor with your God, who will certainly not refuse you.'
Another told me that she *did* believe in Christ, and
prayed to Him every day. I asked her if she also
believed in Gautama, and prayed to him. She replied
that she worshipped them both. I have several times
had my hopes and expectations raised by the appar-
ent seriousness of several women, as Mr. Judson has
had in regard to several men; but their goodness was
like the morning cloud and early dew, which soon
passeth away. Four or five children have committed
the catechism to memory, and often repeat it to each
other."

In November, 1817, the missionaries were joined
by Messrs. Wheelock and Coleman, two additional
missionaries from Boston, America. In December of
the same year, Mr. Judson was forced by a breakdown in his health, on account of over-study of the
language, to leave Rangoon for a sea voyage. The
vessel was bound for Chittagong, in Arakan, but
being caught by contrary winds, she became unman-
ageable in the difficult navigation along that coast.
Her direction was therefore changed for Madras, but
the vessel was borne to a spot three hundred miles
distant from that city, so that Mr. Judson was compelled to travel to Madras by land. Once in Madras,
he was detained until the 20th of July of the next year
before he could return to his wife and work in Rangoon. Worse even than this; on account of the impos-
sibility of communicating with his wife, Mr. Judson
could send no tidings of his whereabouts, so that she

had to endure all the agonies of uncertainty for over six months. And, as if to add to her trouble, persecution broke out in Rangoon, and all foreign priests were ordered to quit the country. It had long been the law of the land that any Burman embracing a foreign faith should pay for his apostasy from Buddhism with his life, and as the friendly Viceroy who had favored the Judsons had been removed to make way for another and more tyrannical official, this law was imperatively announced to the trembling natives and equally helpless missionaries.

Indeed, under Divine providence, Mrs. Judson's firmness and faith alone saved the mission from abandonment at this stage. It seems that almost immediately after the arrival of the news from Chittagong that Mr. Judson had not been heard of at that port, a peremptory and menacing order arrived at the mission house, requiring Mr. Hough, the missionary printer, to appear before the court, and to give an account of himself. He was informed that "if he did not tell all the truth relative to his situation in the country, they would write with his heart's blood." The examination was conducted with such roughness and studied insult that it was very evident mischief was intended; and to complicate the matter still further, Mr. Hough could not speak the language fluently enough to carry on any conversation. Mr. Hough and Mrs. Judson resolved to appeal to the Viceroy, and Mrs. Judson's teacher drew up a petition which she tremblingly presented, somewhat like

Esther of old, when she pleaded for the lives of her people. This petition was successful beyond expectation, for the Viceroy—in spite of the fact that no women were allowed to appear at his court, except by special favor of his wife—commanded that Mr. Hough should receive no futher molestation.

This trouble was over; but the darker one yet remained. No tidings of her husband had yet arrived, and Mr. Hough, believing that the little attack they had experienced was only the first monition of a dark time of persecution, was anxiously eager that Mrs. Judson should accompany him and his family to Bengal. She partly complied with his wish, and even went on board, but returned again to the post of duty, determined to trust herself and her affairs to God's love and keeping. The story is best told by herself in a letter to home friends:

"On the fifth of this month I embarked with Mr. Hough and family for Bengal, having previously disposed of what I could not take with me. I had engaged Mr. Judson's teacher to accompany me, that in case of meeting him at Bengal, he could go on with his Burmese studies. But the teacher, fearing the difficulties arising from his being a Burman, broke his engagement and refused to go. My disinclination to proceed in the course commenced had increased to such a degree that I was on the point of giving up the voyage myself; but my passage was paid, my baggage on board, and I knew not how to separate myself from the mission family. The vessel, however,

was several days in going down the river. When on
the point of putting out to sea, the captain and officers ascertained that she was in a very dangerous
state, in consequence of having been improperly
loaded, and that she must be detained for a day or two
at the place where she then lay. I immediately resolved on giving up the voyage, and returning to
town. Accordingly, the captain sent up a boat with
me, and engaged to forward my baggage the next day.
I reached town in the evening, and to-day have come
out to the mission house, to the great joy of all the
Burmese left on the premises. Mr. Hough and his
family will proceed, and they kindly and affection-
ately urge my going with them. I know I am surrounded by dangers on every hand, and expect to see
much anxiety and distress; but at present I am tran-
quil, and intend to make an effort to pursue my
studies as formerly, and leave the result to God."

The result proved that Mrs. Judson was right. In a
few days Mr. Judson arrived home unexpectedly, to
the rejoicing of his brave wife, and soon after two
new missionaries arrived from America to reinforce
the mission. Then she realized again, with a new
thankfulness, the truth of the lines which she had so
often sung in her fatherland:

> The Lord can clear the darkest skies,
>   Can give us day for night,
> Make drops of sacred sorrow rise
>   To rivers of delight.

Soon after this a preaching-place was opened, and public worship in the Burmese language commenced for all who would attend. In one part of the building, divided off, Mrs. Judson held her class of native women, while in the other Mr. Judson preached, and talked, and argued, attracting congregations, more or less in number, on every day in the week. Inquirers came forward too, asking secretly to be taught all about the new religion, and one—Moung Nau by name—requested baptism as an earnest believer in the Lord Jesus. It may be of help to the reader to know that the prefix *Moung* signifies a young man. The Burmese use a number of titles to designate individuals, like ourselves. Thus, *Moung* denotes a young man; *Do*, an old man; *Mee*, a girl; *Mah*, a young woman; *May*, an old woman. Moung Nau was a young man of about thiry-five years of age, belonging to the middle ranks of life, and evidently much in earnest. It was after about two months of constant instruction that Moung Nau requested baptism—a most thorough proof of his sincerity, when it is considered that he thereby exposed himself to the risk of execution, through forsaking the old religion of the country.

Moung wrote a manly and intelligent letter to Mr. Judson, respecting the rite of baptism sought by him; and because of its straightforward simplicity, as well as its somewhat peculiar phraseology to English readers, we make no apology for reproducing it. The letter runs thus:

"I, Moung Nau, the constant recipient of your excellent favour, now approach your feet. Whereas my lords three [the three missionaries] have come to the country of Burma not for the purposes of trade, but to preach the religion of Jesus Christ, the Son of the eternal God, I, having heard and understood, am with a joyful mind filled with love. I believe that the Divine Son, Jesus Christ, suffered death in the place of men, to atone for their sins. Like a heavy-laden man, I feel my sins are very many. The punishment of my sins I deserve to suffer. Since it is so, do you, sirs, consider that I, taking refuge in the merits of the Lord Jesus Christ, and receiving baptism in order that I may confess myself to be His disciple, shall dwell one with yourselves in the happiness of heaven, and therefore grant me the ordinance of baptism. It is through the grace of Jesus Christ that you, sirs, have come by ship from one country and continent to another, and that we have met together. I pray, my lords three, that a suitable day be appointed, and that I may receive the ordinance of baptism. Moreover, as it is only since I have met you, sirs, that I have known about the eternal God, I venture to pray that you will still unfold to me the religion of God, that my old disposition may be destroyed, and my new disposition improved."

This man was baptized on the 27th of June, 1819. It was the first profession of the Christian faith made by any of the subjects of the Burmese Empire, and it was an occasion of unutterable joy to the missionaries. They had long labored in depression and gloom, while yet sowing precious seed in faith; now Moung Nau was the first sheaf of the harvest. Soon after this two others were baptized, but at sunset, as they were timid believers, and did not desire to proclaim their faith to a numerous concourse of onlookers. After the ceremony, the converts and inquirers repaired to the *Zayat*, and held prayer meetings *of their own accord*. This was a most encouraging sign.

But the unfriendliness and opposition of those in authority increased, so that the natives ceased to come to Mr. Judson or his wife for religious conversation. It seemed certain that it would be useless to persevere in their missionary labors unless they secured the favor of the King; they resolved therefore to visit the capital, endeavor to propitiate his Majesty, and if possible to win his influence over to their side. Messrs. Judson and Colman were admitted to an audience of the King, but their petition was received with disfavor, and their offerings of books rejected with disdain. They returned to Rangoon, dispirited and downcast. They found that the policy of the Burmese Government, in regard to the toleration of any foreign religion, was precisely the same as that of the Chinese; that no subject of the King who embraced a religion different from his own would be exempt from punishment; and that the missionaries in presenting a petition to the sovereign relating to religious toleration had been guilty of a most serious blunder. As a proof, Mr. Judson was informed that some fifteen years previously a native who had been converted to Roman Catholicism had been nearly beaten to death, because of his apostasy from the national faith. The ruling powers entertained still the same spirit of hatred to Protestantism; therefore it seemed hopeless to endeavor to sow gospel seed in or near the capital.

On returning to Rangoon, the saddened mission workers told the three converts of their ill-success, but to their great surprise they found that these men were firm and unmoved in prospect of persecuting days. The only thing which seemed to disquiet them was the probability that the missionaries would leave their country, so that they, being left alone, would be unable to propagate the Christian faith. More especially was this the argument of the married convert; for the two unmarried ones would have followed Mr. Judson to India, whereas the married one could not, because no native woman was permitted to leave the country. It was finally determined that Mr. and Mrs. Colman should remove to Chittagong, and that Mr. and Mrs. Judson should remain with their beloved Burmese hearers, and dare all risks. In March, 1820, the Colmans removed as arranged, and for some time the Judsons labored on bravely alone.

Within a month from the date of the departure of Mr. and Mrs. Colman another convert was baptized, and several native women professed to have received the faith of Christ. The harvest was now beginning to appear after a dreary waiting-time, but had the devoted servants of the Master given way to their very natural feelings of alarm, and fled the country, these converts would probably never have been heard of. In June, however, Mrs. Judson experienced such a breakdown in health that it was deemed absolutely necessary for her to go to Bengal for proper medical treatment. This event, which caused Mr. and Mrs. Judson to leave Burma, became the means of leading other natives to come forward and make profession of faith, and among them was Mah-Men-la, one of Mrs. Judson's women scholars. She was baptized upon her confession of faith, saying, "Now I have taken the oath of allegiance to Jesus Christ, and I have nothing to do but to commit myself, soul and body, into the hands of my Lord, assured that He will never suffer me to fall away."

The voyage and treatment benefited Mrs. Judson so much that, in January, 1821, she and her husband returned from Serampore to Rangoon, and were welcomed by all classes. Even the wife of the Viceroy received the missionaries with unwonted friendliness, but the most cheering fact of all was this, that though they were left to themselves for above six months, not one of the converts had dishonored the Christian profession. Owing to the great caution observed, the little church had dwelt amidst many and powerful enemies at Rangoon quite unmolested. Mr. Judson records that it was not then generally known that any of the natives had professed Christianity. It was the day of small things, and whether the religion of the Cross should ever spread over the benighted land of Burma was at that time an unsolved problem.

A village on stilts

6

Dark Days

IN MAY, 1821, the American Baptist Missionary Society set apart and sent out Dr. Price to assist Mr. and Mrs. Judson. The Doctor was married, and having received a medical education was prepared to act both as missionary and medical man. But cholera and fever were their constant foes; and what with translation, teaching, preaching, and disputing, the days passed very quickly to both Mr. and Mrs. Judson until it became too evident that the health of the latter was being surely undermined by constant suffering from fever and liver complaint. It being painfully recognized that there existed no chance of her recovery in those Eastern climes, it was at last decided that she should pay a visit to America. In August, therefore, she embarked for Bengal, and after arriving in Calcutta in the following month she made further arrangements for visiting England *en route* for the United States. On writing to a friend she thus referred to her departure from Burma:

"Rangoon, from having been the theatre in which so much of the faithfulness, power, and mercy of God has been exhibited, from having been considered for ten years past my home for life, and from a thousand interesting associations, has become the dearest spot on earth. Hence you will readily imagine that no ordinary considerations could have induced my departure . . . .

"I left Rangoon in August, and arrived in Calcutta on the 22nd of September. My disorder gained ground so rapidly that nothing but a voyage to sea, and the benefit of the cold climate, presented the least hope of life. You will also realise that nothing else than the prospect of a final separation would have induced us to decide on this measure, under circumstances so trying as those in which we were placed. But duty to God, to ourselves, to the Board of Missions, and to the perishing Burmese, compelled us to adopt this course of procedure, though agonising to all the natural feelings of our hearts."

Mrs. Judson made arrangements to go to England first, solely because of the difficulty of engaging a passage in any American vessel; and as it turned out, she was able to do this, free of expense to the Board. She continued: "If the pain in my side is entirely removed while on my passage to Europe, I shall return to India in the same ship, and proceed immediately to Rangoon. But if not, I shall go over to America, and spend one winter in my dear native country. As ardently as I long to see my beloved friends in America, I cannot prevail on myself to be any longer from Rangoon than is absolutely necessary for the preservation of my life. I have had a severe struggle relative to my *immediate* return to Rangoon, instead of going to England. But I did not venture to go contrary to the convictions of reason, to the opinion of an eminent and skilful physician, and the repeated injunctions of Mr. Judson."

She reached England with somewhat improved health, and at once found a welcome among Christians of all denominations. After spending some weeks among English and Scottish friends, she proceeded in August, 1822, on her way to New York, arriving there on the 25th of September. She intended to have spent the winter in the New England States, but the coldness of the climate and her own exhaustion of strength forbade this plan being carried out. She therefore removed to Baltimore in December, this place being more suitable to her constitution after the tropical heat of Burma. It is somewhat saddening to know, however, that the malignancy of poor human nature found vent in unworthy misrepresentations of Mrs. Judson's character and conduct during this winter. It was asserted by some envious and detracting persons that her health was not seriously impaired, and that she only visited the Southern States with a view to attracting attention and applause. But such detraction was not at all to be wondered at, seeing that the disciples of Christ must ever expect the same baptism of ill-will, defamation, and slander through which He passed. No Christian, indeed, who has been worth the name, has ever incurred the "woe" denounced on those of whom all the world shall "speak well"; and in passing through this experience, Mrs. Judson merely suffered like all the rest of Christ's disciples.

During the winter at Baltimore frequent consultations of medical men took place, and they all concurred in thinking that she could not expect to live if she returned to Burma, or indeed to the East at all. But she still anticipated the time of her departure for the scene of missionary toils and triumphs, and expressed herself determined to labor for Burma as long as life should last. Yet her illness increased, and alarming complications ensued. Bleeding from the lungs came on in addition to liver symptoms, and for some time it grew even doubtful whether she would recover sufficiently ever to take the long voyage back. Meanwhile, encouraging reports arrived from Rangoon. The little band of native women whom she had been instructing there had nearly all given in their adhesion to Christianity, or had been baptized, and were actually carrying on a small prayer meeting *of their own accord.* Dr. Price had received the Burmese monarch's command to repair to Ava on account of his medical skill, and Mr. Judson had resolved to accompany him in order to make one more effort to accompany him in order to make one more effort for toleration for the native Christians. These things made Mrs. Judson anxious to return to Rangoon early in April, should a vessel be sailing from either Boston or Salem.

During this waiting-time she published the *History of the Burman Mission,* a small work, but a valuable compilation of facts, which drew much attention to the condition of the country from both American and English Christians. As one result, doubtless, of the increased interest excited, the American Board of Missions appointed Mr. and Mrs. Wade to proceed to Burma with Mrs. Judson, to assist in the mission there. The little party sailed from Boston on the 22nd of June, and after a prosperous voyage, arrived at Rangoon *via* Calcutta, on the 5th of December, 1823. But Mrs. Judson found that serious complications, endangering the safety of the mission, had arisen in her absence. Indeed, there can be little doubt that the cloud was now appearing, "small as a man's hand," which was destined to end only with her death. The difficulties and hardships she had hitherto experienced were few and small compared with those which now awaited her.

The new Viceroy of Rangoon was opposed to Christianity, and manifested his spirit by imposing illegal and burdensome taxes upon every Burmese suspected of favoring the principles taught by Mr. Judson. The houses of some of the disciples were demolished, and they themselves were gone, no one knew whither, for they had fled for dear life. The prospect of war between England and Burma was daily increasing; therefore the missionaries who had been occupying the land during her absence had a tale to tell of gloomy anticipation and lowering evil. Dr. Price was resident at Ava, the "Golden City," having been commanded to remain there because of his medical skill; and Mr. Judson had also to take up his residence there because of some passing mood of indulgence or of toleration in the Imperial mind. Mrs. Judson's next home was therefore to be at Ava, several hundred miles farther up the Irrawaddy.

Immediately on her arrival therefore at Rangoon, Mr. Judson prepared to take her up the Irrawaddy to Ava, for the Emperor's behests could not be disregarded without fear of trouble. This state of matters, however, divided the mission party, one half being driven to reside in Ava, in the very teeth of danger, and the other half being left behind at Rangoon. The party at the capital consisted of Messrs. Judson and Price, with their families; that at Rangoon of Messrs. Hough and Wade, and their families. These two missionaries suffered much persecution and illtreatment during the progress of the war, but still their sufferings were very little indeed compared with those of the Judsons and Dr. Price. Mrs. Price, before this climax arrived, found an early grave among those whom she sought to benefit.

The voyage up the Irrawaddy took about six weeks, and was performed in Mr. Judson's small open boat, but as the season was cool and healthy, the voyagers performed the journey pleasantly and easily. The river banks were peopled by swarms of human beings, all anxious to get a peep at "the white woman from over the water"; and all wondering, when they did get a peep at her, how she could ever muster up sufficient courage to visit their land. Whenever the boat came to a halt for the night, Mr. and Mrs. Judson would get out, and sit in the shade of the trees; then a crowd would soon gather, to whom Mr. Judson would talk simply of the great and loving Saviour, Christ. He also seized these opportunities to distribute tracts, printed in Burmese, containing short and simple statements of Christian doctrine, which tracts were eagerly received and willingly read, for most of the Burmese could read their own language, and were fairly fond of discussing religious questions with the missionaries.

On arriving at Ava, they had to wait about a fortnight while a little wooden house was run up for them. It contained three small rooms and a verandah, and was raised on supports four feet from the ground. But as the house was not built of bricks, its inhabitants soon began to suffer from the intense heat. Mrs. Judson writes: "I hardly know how we shall bear the hot season which is just commencing, as our house is built of boards, and before night is heated like an oven. Nothing but brick is a shelter from the heat of Ava, when the thermometer, even in the shade, frequently rises to 108 degrees. We have worship every evening in Burmese, when a number of the natives assemble; and every Sabbath, Mr. Judson preaches on the other side of the river, in Dr. Price's house. We feel it an inestimable privilege that, amid all our discouragements, we have the language, and are able constantly to communicate truths which can save the soul."

But the war-clouds loomed dark in the distance, and threatened, at no distant date, to overwhelm them and the whole mission in ruin. Indeed, although unknown to them, "the dogs of war" had been already let loose. For some time past rumors of approaching war with the Bengal Government had disturbed the public security. It had been known for a long period that the Emperor of Burma had cherished the ambitious design of invading Bengal. He had collected, in a neighboring province, an army of 30,000 men, under the command of one of his most successful generals. It was also said that this army was furnished with a pair of golden fetters, wherewith to bind the Governor-General of India, when he should be led away into captivity in Burma.

But these preparations for triumph over a fallen foe were destined to premature failure as in many another case. The British rulers of India, as represented by the Bengal Government, decided to invade Burma, and at once to administer exemplary punishment in return for the encroachments and insults of the Burmese Government. All peaceable measures had been tried and failed; now it only remained to appeal by force of arms.

In May, 1824—or about five months after Mrs. Judson's return—an army of ten thousand British and East Indian Troops, under the command of Sir Archibald Campbell, arrived at Rangoon. This was about three months after Mr. and Mrs. Judson had arrived at their new home at Ava. The army struck terror into the hearts of the people at Rangoon, and the Viceroy revenged himself upon Messrs. Hough and Wade by inflicting cruel treatment, and threatening them with death. He pretended to believe that the Americans were in league with the English, and treated them accordingly. These two missionaries were thrust into prison, loaded with fetters, and more than once brought out for instant execution. The landing of the British troops finally saved them from death; and after a while, both Messrs. Hough and Wade, with their wives, returned to Bengal, where they still carried on the work of translating and printing, as far as manuscript had been prepared. Mr. Wade chiefly employed himself in printing a Burmese dictionary, which had been prepared by Mr. Judson, and which proved to be a work of much value to later missionaries.

But the tide of war rolled on to Ava, and the situation of the missionaries there became a matter of intense solicitude, not only to their fellow-workers, but also to the friends of the mission in America. Nothing had been heard of the Judsons or of Dr. Price for nearly two years, and at last even their nearest and dearest friends gave them up for dead. It was certain that, if alive, they were suffering bitter pains and persecutions for their supposed connection with the British, while it was almost equally certain that as the British troops proceeded from victory to victory, the Burmese authorities would wreak their vengeance upon the defenseless missionaries who were all this time in their power.

At last, however, the British advanced so near the capital that Sir Archibald Campbell was able to dictate terms of peace, and the Burmese monarch was glad to comply. He agreed to cede a large portion of his territory, to pay about one million sterling, in four instalments, and to liberate unconditionally all the British and American prisoners. Mr. and Mrs. Judson, as well as Dr. Price, were thus rescued from the hands of their enemies, and on the 24th of February, 1826, they were received with the most courteous kindness at the British camp. Sir Archibald Campbell provided the missionaries with a tent, and also placed one of his gun-boats at their disposal, to convey them down the river Irrawaddy to Rangoon, whenever they decided to go. At this date Mrs. Judson was so weak with fever, hardship, and Burmese brutality that she could not stand or walk without support, yet she looked forward to being of some use to the benighted Burmese, provided she could settle down in some other part of Burma, under British protection.

Mrs. Judson wrote a complete account of their

sufferings during this terrible time. Of this account it has been well said, "Fiction itself has seldom invented a tale more replete with terror." From it we learn that their sorrows began immediately on their arrival at Ava, for Dr. Price was out of favor at the Burmese court, while all foreigners were looked upon with suspicion, as being naturally favorable to the British. As soon as the tidings of the capture of Rangoon reached Ava, an order was issued that all foreigners should be cast into prison. The storm burst upon the household of the Judsons on the 8th of June, 1824, just as they were preparing for dinner. Mrs. Judson thus describes the scene:

"In rushed an officer, holding a black book, with a dozen Burmese, accompanied by one whom from his spotted face we knew to be the executioner, and 'a son of the prison.' 'Where is the teacher?' was the first inquiry. Mr. Judson presented himself. 'You are called by the Emperor,' said the officer, a form of speech always used when about to arrest a criminal. The spotted man instantly seized Mr. Judson, threw him on the floor, and produced the small cord, the instrument of torture. I caught hold of his arm. 'Stay,' said I, 'I will give you money.' *'Take her too,'* said the officer, *'she also is a foreigner.'* Mr. Judson, with an imploring look, begged that they would let me remain till further orders. The scene was now shocking beyond description. The whole neighborhood had collected: the masons at work on the brick house threw down their tools, and ran; the little Burmese children were screaming and crying, the servants stood in amazement at the indignities offered their master, and the hardened executioner, with a kind of insane joy, drew tight the cords, bound Mr. Judson fast, and dragged him off, I knew not whither. In vain I begged and entreated the spotted-face to take the silver, and loosen the ropes, but he spurned my offers, and immediately departed. I gave the money, however, to Moung Ing to follow after, and make some attempt to mitigate the torture of Mr. Judson, but instead of succeeding, the unfeeling wretches, when a few rods from the house, again threw their prisoners on the ground, and drew the cords still tighter, so as almost to prevent respiration."

A guard of ten ruffians was set over the house, and Mrs. Judson was closely watched, together with the little Burmese girls whom she had taken to teach and train up in her own family. Very soon, however, she was summoned forth to the verandah to be examined by the magistrate for supposed complicity with the British foreigners. Previous to obeying this summons, however, she took the precaution of destroying all her letters, journals, and writings of every kind, lest they should disclose the fact that they had correspondents in England. After the examination, she was allowed to retire to an inner room with the children; but the carousings and vile language of the guard, her own suffering, unprotected, and desolate state, as well as the uncertainty of her husband's fate, combined to render it a most memorable night of terror and dismay, sleep being altogether out of the question.

She sent Moung Ing, however, early next morning to ascertain Mr. Judson's situation, and if possible, to give him and his fellow-prisoner food. He soon returned with the tidings that both the missionaries, with all the white foreigners, were confined in the death-prison, with three pairs of iron fetters each, and fastened to a long pole to prevent their moving. The fact of being a prisoner herself rendered it impossible to take any effectual steps for their release. She did try, however, what could be done, by sending letters, messages, and promises of rewards to various high officials and members of the royal family, but all her endeavors were unsuccessful. She had obtained permission at last, upon paying about one hundred dollars to the head officer, to have one short interview with her husband; but when Mr. Judson crawled to the door of the prison, and commenced to give her directions as to her efforts for his release, the jailers roughly compelled her to depart, with threats of personal violence.

Next, the officers of the Burmese Government visited Mr. Judson's house and coolly proceeded to take possession of all they had. But, very fortunately, Mrs. Judson had received warning of this visit of confiscation, and had on the previous day secreted as much silver as she possibly could, knowing that if the

war lasted long, she and the other missionaries would
be reduced to utter starvation. Although the Burmese Government held them all as prisoners, it was
considered a superfluous duty to feed them. No
trouble whatever was taken either to provide mats or
food for Mr. Judson or Dr. Price; consequently Mrs.
Judson had regularly to send them food, together
with mats to sleep upon. Only books, medicines, and
wearing apparel were left in her possession now, so
that had she not taken the precaution to hide their
money, she and the prisoners would have perished of
starvation. Her almost daily journeys to the prison,
however, which was two miles away, and her exhaust-
ing interviews with officials, greatly reduced her own
strength. This went on for seven months, until her
resources and her courage were both alike nearly
exhausted. The extortions and oppressions they had
to bear are quite indescribable, and the awful uncertainty of their fate was overpowering. Mrs. Judson
says, in her account of this terrible time, "My prevail-
ing opinion was that my husband would suffer a
violent death, and that I should of course become a
slave, and languish out a miserable, though short,
existence in the hands of some unfeeling monster."

To add to the difficulties of the lonely woman's
situation, she gave birth to a little daughter after Mr.
Judson had been some time in prison. This babe
comforted her heart a little, but it also added to her
cares and duties. As often as possible, she would take
it to the death-prison, in order that its father might

look upon it, and we can well believe that the little unconscious infant, although by her tiny baby wiles serving to bring some ray of pleasure to the poor prisoner's heart, would cause a pang to pierce through that heart as it contemplated the dark and unknown future.

Sometimes, however, Mr. Judson suffered with fever, and was in great danger; but once, as a special favor, his wife was permitted to erect a small bamboo house in the governor's enclosure, opposite the prison gate, and to remove her husband into it. She was also allowed to go in and out at all times of the day, to administer medicines to him, and she adds: "I now feel happy indeed—although the little bamboo hovel was so low that neither of us could stand upright."

But worse experiences were to come. One morning, when Mr. Judson was still ill with fever, he and the other white prisoners were taken out of the prison, and driven on foot some eight or ten miles, under the burning sun, both bareheaded and barefooted, to Amarapura. This cross-country march was so dreadful that one of the white prisoners—a Greek—dropped dead.

At first nobody could tell Mrs. Judson where the poor captives were taken, but a servant who had witnessed the forced march brought her information. Nothing daunted, this devoted woman followed her husband, carrying her infant in her arms, accompanied by her two little Burmese girls and a faithful

Bengali cook. Part of the journey was accomplished in a boat, and part in a rough country cart. She found Mr. Judson and his companions chained in couples with fetters, and almost dead from fever, exhaustion, and want. She says: "It was now dark; I had no refreshment for the suffering prisoners, or for myself, as I had expected to procure all that was necessary at the market of Amarapura, and I had no shelter for the night. I asked one of the jailers if I might put up a little bamboo house near the prison; he said, 'No, it was not customary.' I then begged he would procure me a shelter for the night, when on the morrow I would find some place to live in. He took me to his house, in which there were only two small rooms —one in which he and his family lived—the other, which was then half full of grain, he offered to me, and in that little filthy place I spent the next six months of wretchedness. I procured some half-boiled water instead of tea, and worn out with fatigue, laid myself down on a mat spread over the grain, and endeavoured to obtain a little refreshment from sleep."

The prisoners, meanwhile, were confined in an old shattered building without a roof, and the rumor went forth that they were to be burned alive, building and all. It came out afterwards, indeed, that had it not been for the death of the officer whose duty it would have been to see them burned, they would have perished in this dreadful manner.

Just at that juncture, as if to add woe upon woe, the

little Burmese girls took the smallpox, and shortly afterwards the infant sickened with it too, in spite of the fact that Mrs. Judson vaccinated it, as best she could, with an old darning-needle. It however had only a slight attack in consequence of the vaccination; but, what with children to vaccinate, the little ones of her own family to nurse, and Mr. Judson to care and cook for, Mrs. Judson had her hands full. She had also to make a journey to Ava for medicines, and this journey, together with the exhaustion, anxiety, and hardships of her life, combined to lay her also low with malignant fever. During this time the Bengali cook was most faithful, and served both his master and mistress night and day with unremitting fidelity; and sometimes the jailers would allow Mr. Judson to come out of prison to nurse his wife and babe for a few hours. She tells us that for want of proper nursing the infant had grown to be a "little emaciated creature," while "her cries were heart-rending."

Soon after, Mr. Judson was released from captivity and ordered to proceed to the Burmese camp, to act as translator and interpreter in the negotiations then being carried on with Sir Archibald Campbell for peace. The British Army advanced upon Ava, and in order to save the city, the Burmese King agreed to the most humiliating stipulations. Mr. Judson and Dr. Price were sent forward to sue for peace. They brought back the message that the British would spare the city, provided the Burmese Government would pay one million sterling, and immediately liberate all foreign prisoners. After some haggling these conditions were accepted, and Sir Archibald Campbell received the whole of the prisoners, and entertained them in his own camp with every mark of respect.

During these negotiations for peace, Mrs. Judson was very ill with spotted fever. Her hair was shaved off, her head and feet covered with blisters, and she was so far gone that the Burmese who came in to sit by her said to one another, *"She is dead."* She however rallied, but it was more than a month before she could stand.

At that time the Judsons had no idea of ever being able to leave Ava, not having the remotest notion that the British General would include them in his demands. But still the result proved better than their fears. Upon their arrival at the British camp, Mrs. Judson says, "Sir Archibald took us to his own table, and treated us with the kindness of a father, rather than as strangers. I presume to say that no persons on earth were ever happier than we were during the fortnight we passed at the British camp. For several days this idea wholly occupied my mind, that we were out of the power of the Burmese Government, and once more under the protection of the British. Our feelings continually dictated expressions like these, 'What shall we render to the Lord for all His benefits?' "

7

Called Home

THERE IS AN INTERESTING FACT regarding Mr. Judson's manuscript translation of the New Testament which deserves to be recorded. When at the commencement of this long season of suffering the Burmese Government officials went to the Judsons' house for the purpose of seizing all their property, Mrs. Judson, instead of burning the Testament together with the letters and journals, hid it in the earth. Unfortunately, however, it was the rainy season, and the manuscript ran the risk of being destroyed by damp. She therefore dug it up, and stitched it into the pillow, so dirty and mean that, as she supposed, not even a native official would be likely to covet it. Mr. Judson slept on it for some time, but was ultimately robbed of it by one of the officials, who, after stripping off the outer covering, threw away the pillow itself, because it was so hard. One of the native converts, happening to be passing by, picked it up, took care of it, and months afterward restored the precious manuscript to Mr. Judson intact.

In the beginning of May, 1826, the Judsons removed to Amherst, a new city under British protection. Four of the mission converts, with their families, had already settled there, besides many of the Burmese population, so that there was every prospect of a new and more successful time of service. But Mrs. Judson's work was almost accomplished. In July, Mr. Judson was summoned away to assist in negotiating a secondary treaty between the British and the Burmese, which was to secure toleration for Christianity, and establish peace on a firm basis. This was the final parting between husband and wife.

Before his return Mrs. Judson was seized again with malignant fever, and her shattered constitution was unable to withstand its attacks. The terrible sufferings she had passed through at Ava rendered her an easy prey. The surgeons and officers of the British regiment stationed at Amherst did all in their power to alleviate the sickness; and the wife of one of the men acted as nurse, most kindly and unremittingly. But Mrs. Judson's strength declined very rapidly and her mind wandered; still the salvation of the Burmese people lay near her heart. She seemed to dwell much at intervals upon the idea of seeing her husband once more. One day she moaned out: "The teacher is long in coming, and the new missionaries are long in coming; I must die alone and leave my little one; but as it is the will of God, I acquiesce in His will. I am not afraid of death, but I am afraid I shall not be able to bear these pains. Tell the teacher that the disease was most violent, and that I could not write; tell him how I suffered and died; tell him all that you see; and take care of the house and things till he returns."

The last day or two she lay, almost senseless and motionless, on one side, her head reclining on her arm, her eyes closed, and at eight in the evening of the 24th of October, 1826, she passed into "the better land"—sinking to rest like a weary child. Mr. Judson returned too late to see her lifeless corpse.

She was buried at Amherst with civil and military honors; and a tree was planted near her grave. Afterwards, a monument was sent from Boston to mark the spot. Six months later the infant rejoined its mother, and was laid by her side in the little enclosure.

It certainly was a mysterious dispensation of Providence that Mrs. Judson should be called away from her beloved work just as she had the opportunity of an "open door," and had acquired capability for service. Familiar with the language, and rich in experience, she might, to our thinking, have done very much more service in the mission field. But previous hardships, trials of climate, and deprivation of comforts had all done their work, and "she was not, for the finger of God touched her." However, she had not lived in vain. Five converted Burmese had preceded her to heaven, nearly all of whom had heard the news of redemption from her lips.

Her name will be remembered in the churches of Burma in future times when the pagodas of Gautama shall have fallen; when the spires of Christian temples shall gleam along the waters of the Irrawaddy and the Salween; and when the Golden City shall have "lifted up her gates to let the King of Glory in."

Mr. Judson outlived his wife for twenty-four years, and was permitted to carry on his noble work in Burma until his death in 1850. During the last years of his labors he again saw much antagonism to the gospel from the authorities, but he persevered and what a great monumental work Mr. Judson reared for God amid tremendous difficulties and trials. Not only had he finished the translation of the Bible, but also had completed the larger and more difficult part of the Burmese dictionary. At the time of his death there were sixty-three churches established among the Burmans and Karens. Surely he had laid the foundations of the gospel in Burman hearts which could never be overthrown, and a work was accomplished which shall redound to the glory of God throughout all eternity. He and his noble wife had fought a good fight; they had finished their course; henceforth there is laid up for them a crown of righteousness; and not for them only, but for all who, like them, crown Christ in their hearts as Lord and Saviour, and yield to Him for His service, in absolute surrender and consecration.

In conclusion, it may not be out of place to recount a few encouraging facts concerning the later state of the American Baptist Mission to Burma. Christianity had increased and prospered far more in this land than was generally known. There were six hundred Christian congregations, comprising about twenty-eight thousand members, and about seventy thousand adherents. Thse congregations were, as a rule, self-supporting, and were composed chiefly of Karens. Beside these there were about fifteen hundred Burmese converts. In four hundred schools there were also twelve thousand pupils. The whole Bible was freely circulated in the Burmese tongue as the result of Mr. Judson's labors; to say nothing of the dictionary, hymn book, and thousands of smaller works, such as tracts, pamphlets, and catechisms. There was no system of caste in Burma, such as has been the curse of India, so that access to the different orders of people was more easy; while the majority of the natives could read their own language owing to the system of instruction pursued by the *phoongyes* or priests. It was arranged to build a Judson Centennial Memorial Church in Mandalay, the new capital of Burma, which is near the site of Ava, and only two miles from the dreadful prison of Oung-pen-la where the heroic Judson and his fellow-captive suffered so much torture. Several thousand pounds were required for the erection of this building; but one thousand was given as a starting-gift by Meh-Nhinly, an aged Christian widow, who for many years had been the mainstay of the little Burmese church at Tavoy, and who was one of the very few then still alive who had been baptized by Mr. Judson himself.

More than a century has passed away since Mrs. Judson was laid to rest in that lonely grave at Amherst, but her work still bears fruit. The word of the Lord has not returned to Him void, but has prospered in the work whereunto it was sent, even in idolatrous Burma. It is long past a century since —driven out of Calcutta by the old East India Company—Mr. Judson arrived in Rangoon, and first established the Baptist Mission. For a long time he labored on in the face of discouragements which would have vanquished a less courageous man. But now we may well marvel at the multitude of the harvest fruits! Burma, which has become one of the most valuable possessions of the British Crown, may yet be one of the most enlightened lands owning the sway of "the King of kings."